HANDEL FOR TENOR SAXOPHONE

HANDEL

Wise Publications
London/New York/Paris/Sydney/Copenhagen/Madrid

Exclusive Distributors:
Music Sales Limited
8/9 Frith Street,
London W1V 5TZ, England.

Music Sales Pty Limited
120 Rothschild Avenue,
Rosebery, NSW 2018, Australia.

Music Sales Corporation
257 Park Avenue South,
New York, NY10010, United States of America.

This book © Copyright 1994 by
Wise Publications
Order No. AM92105
ISBN 0-7119-4231-5

Music processed by Interactive Sciences Limited, Gloucester
Designed by Hutton & Partners

Music Sales' complete catalogue describes thousands of titles and is available in full colour sections by subject, direct from Music Sales Limited. Please state your areas of interest and send a cheque/postal order for £1.50 for postage to: Music Sales Limited, Newmarket Road, Bury St. Edmunds, Suffolk IP33 3YB.

Your Guarantee of Quality
As publishers, we strive to produce every book to the highest commercial standards.

The music has been freshly engraved and the book has been carefully designed to minimise awkward page turns and to make playing from it a real pleasure.

Particular care has been given to specifying acid-free, neutral-sized paper made from pulps which have not been elemental chlorine bleached. This pulp is from farmed sustainable forests and was produced with special regard for the environment. Throughout, the printing and binding have been planned to ensure a sturdy, attractive publication which should give years of enjoyment.

If your copy fails to meet our high standards, please inform us and we will gladly replace it.

Unauthorised reproduction of any part of this publication by any means including photocopying is an infringement of copyright.

Printed in the United Kingdom by
Caligraving Limited, Thetford, Norfolk.

CONTENTS

ACIS AND GALATEA
18 Love In Her Eyes

AMADIGI DI GAULA
7 Dance And Trio

BERENICE
22 Minuet

CHANDOS ANTHEM No.5
24 O Magnify The Lord

CONCERTO GROSSO No.12
14 Larghetto

FIREWORKS MUSIC
20 Martial Movement

JUDAS MACCABAEUS
23 O Lovely Peace
27 See The Conquering Hero Comes

MESSIAH
6 But Who May Abide
29 Hallelujah Chorus Themes
8 He Shall Feed His Flock
12 How Beautiful Are The Feet
13 I Know That My Redeemer Liveth
21 Minuet

OBOE CONCERTO No.3 IN G MINOR
26 Sarabande

PTOLOMY
28 Silent Worship

REDEMPTION
9 Holy, Holy
31 Where Is This Stupendous Stranger

RINALDO
16 Lascia Ch'io Pianga

SAMSON
17 Let The Bright Seraphim

SCIPIONE
19 March

SEMELE
30 Where E'er You Walk

SIROE
25 O Placido Il Mare

WATER MUSIC
4 Air
5 Bourrée
10 Hornpipe

XERXES
15 Largo

Air
from Water Music

Bourrée
from Water Music

But Who May Abide
from Messiah

Dance And Trio
from Amadigi di Gaula

Bright tempo

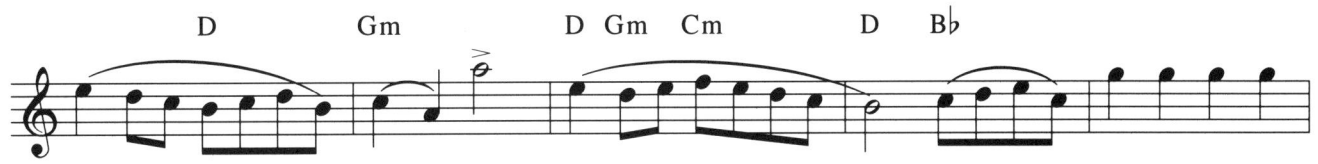
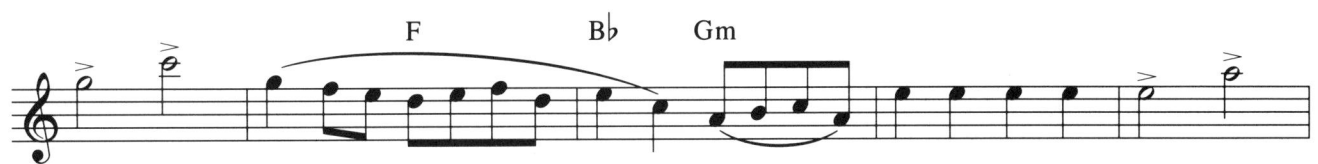
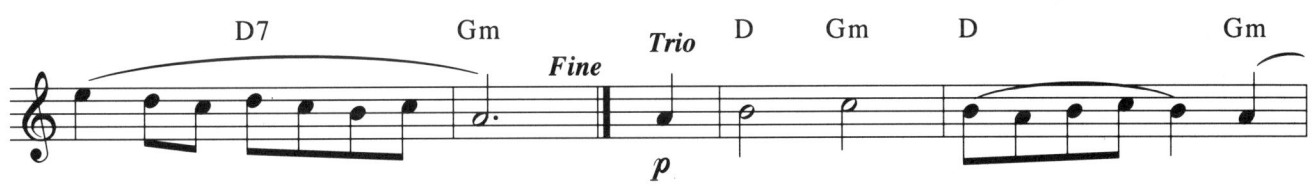
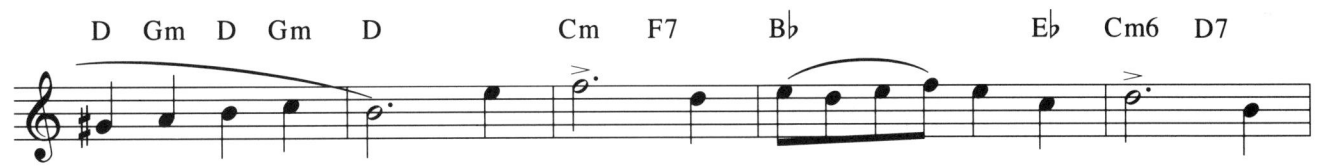

He Shall Feed His Flock
from Messiah

Holy, Holy
from Redemption

Hornpipe
from Water Music

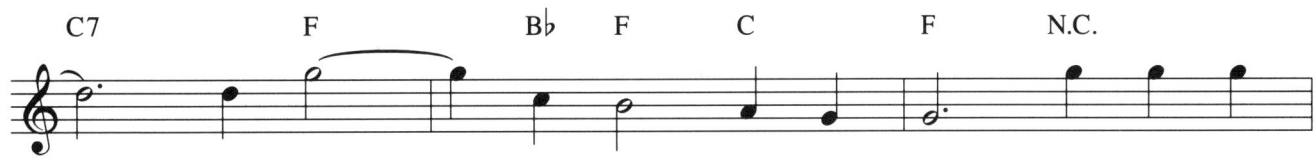

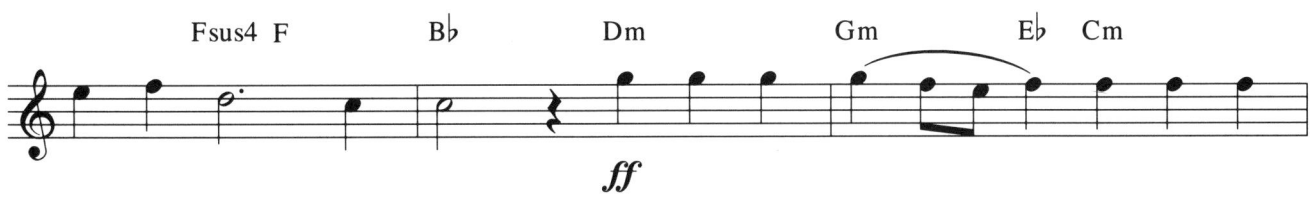
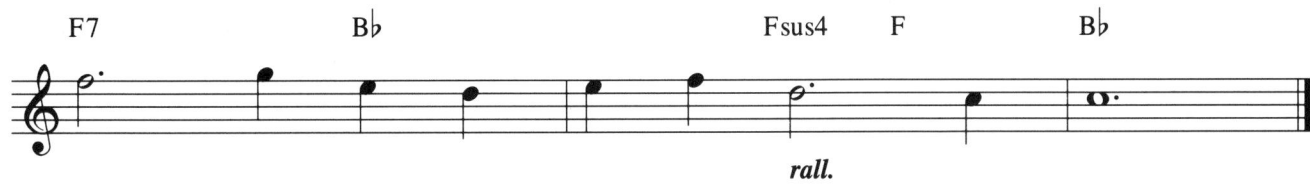

How Beautiful Are The Feet
from Messiah

Moderately slow

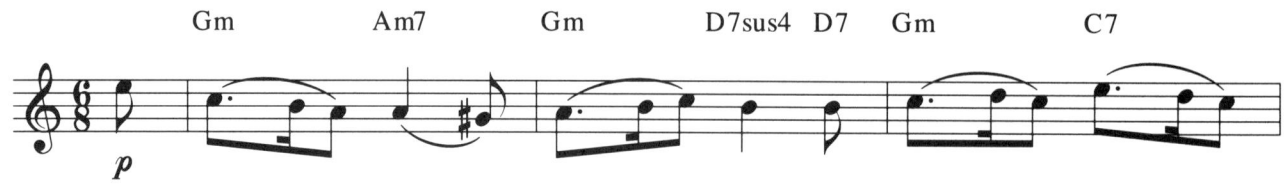
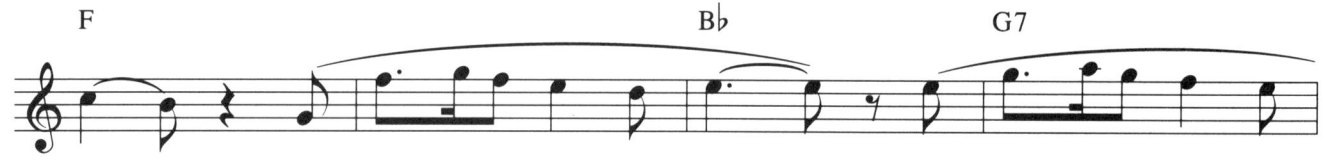
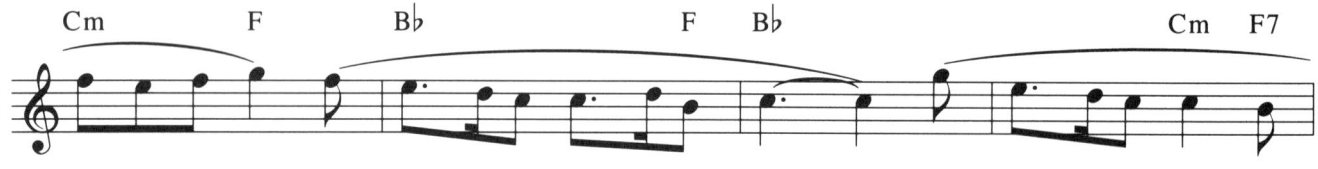

© Copyright 1994 Dorsey Brothers Music Limited, 8/9 Frith Street, London W1.
All Rights Reserved. International Copyright Secured.

I Know That My Redeemer Liveth
from Messiah

Not too slow

Larghetto
from Concerto Grosso No. 12

Largo
from Xerxes

Lascia Ch'io Pianga
from Rinaldo

Let The Bright Seraphim
from Samson

Love In Her Eyes
from Acis and Galatea

March
from Scipione

Martial Movement
from Fireworks Music

Minuet

Moderately

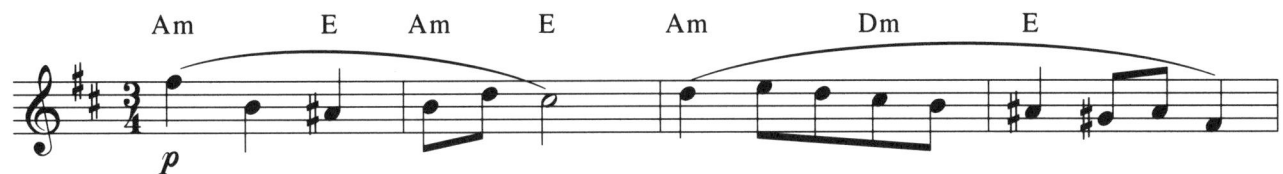

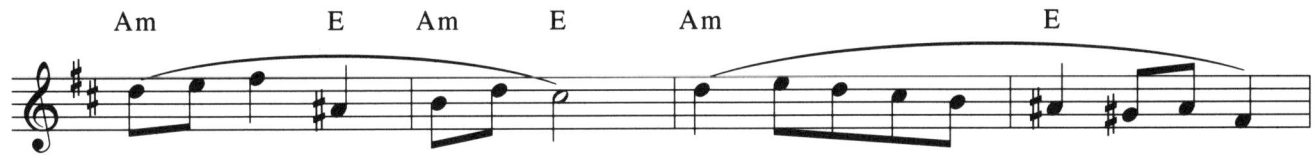

Minuet
from Berenice

Moderately

O Lovely Peace
from Judas Maccabaeus

O Magnify The Lord
from Chandos Anthem No. 5

O Placido Il Mare
from Siroe

Sarabande
from Oboe Concerto No. 3 in G Minor

See The Conquering Hero Comes
from Judas Maccabaeus

Majestically

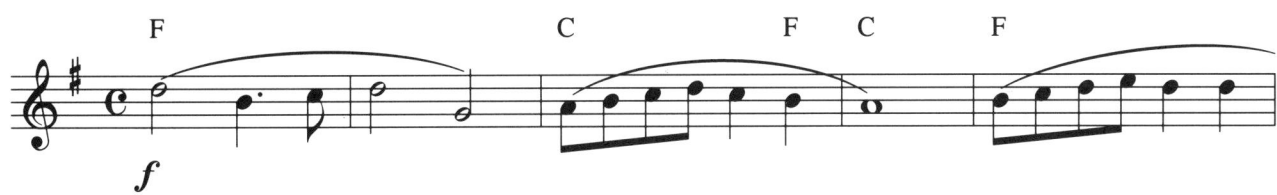
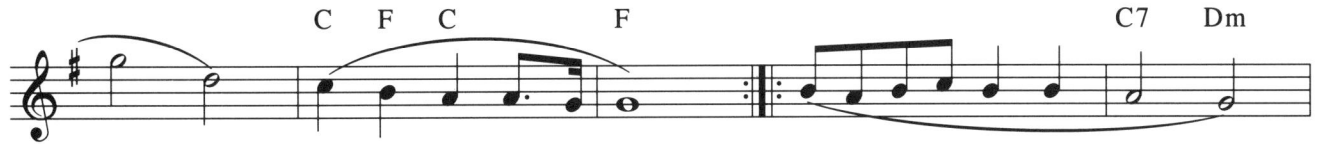

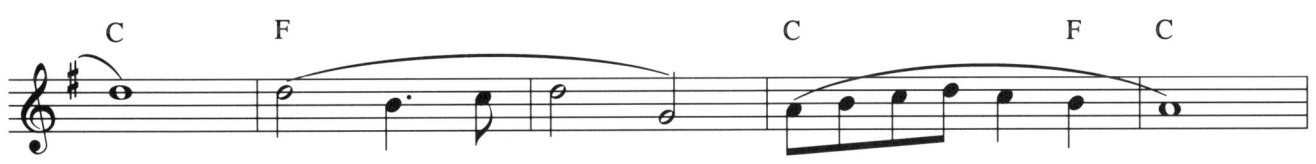
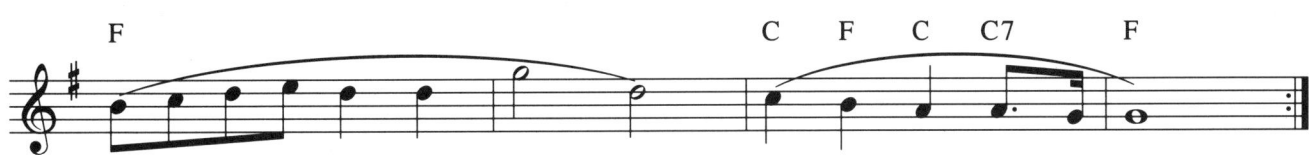

© Copyright 1994 Dorsey Brothers Music Limited, 8/9 Frith Street, London W1.
All Rights Reserved. International Copyright Secured.

Silent Worship
from Ptolomy

Themes from Hallelujah Chorus
from Messiah

Where E'er You Walk
from Semele

Where Is This Stupendous Stranger
from Redemption

The Beatles

Enya

Phil Collins

Van Morrison

Bob Dylan

Sting

Paul Simon

Tracy Chapman

Eric Clapton

Pink Floyd

New Kids On The Block

Bryan Adams

Tina Turner

Elton John

Bee Gees

Whitney Houston

AC/DC

Bringing you the words

All the latest in rock and pop. Plus the brightest and best in West End show scores. Music books for every instrument under the sun. And exciting new teach-yourself ideas like "Let's Play Keyboard" - in cassette/book packs, or on video. Available from all good music shops.

and music

Music Sales' complete catalogue lists thousands of titles and is available free from your local music shop, or direct from Music Sales Limited. Please send a cheque or postal order for £1.50 (for postage) to:

Music Sales Limited
Newmarket Road,
Bury St Edmunds,
Suffolk IP33 3YB

Buddy

Five Guys Named Moe

Les Misérables

West Side Story

Phantom Of The Opera

Show Boat

The Rocky Horror Show

Bringing you the world's best music.